Connecticut Joins the Revolution

THE CONNECTICUT REVOLUTION BICENTENNIAL BOOKLETS
AN INTRODUCTION TO THE SERIES

In the early 1930's, Connecticut celebrated the tercentenary of her founding with a series of pamphlets dealing with many phases of the State's history. There are, in all, sixty pamphlets—some prepared by the most eminent authorities in their fields. Several of the contributions to the *Tercentenary Pamphlet Series* are still, despite the considerable lapse of time, the best work on the subject. Many of the titles are still in print, and most of those of which the original Yale University Press printing has been exhausted have been re-issued by the Connecticut State Library.

It was the remarkable success of the pamphlet series that prompted the American Revolution Bicentennial Commission of Connecticut to publish the *Connecticut Revolution Bicentennial Booklets*. Obviously, the *Pamphlets* provide the model for the *Booklets*, but there are significant ways in which the two differ. The *Booklets* are, first of all, limited in period to what the Bicentennial Commission has broadly defined as the Revolutionary Era—1763 to 1787. Emphasis will be placed upon the birth of the nation, rather than on the winning of independence on the field of battle. Each *Booklet* will be roughly twice the length of the average *Pamphlet*, with most numbers running from 60 to 75 pages. In each instance, every effort has been made to secure the most highly qualified author, and this, the reader will doubtless confirm, has happily been achieved.

Thus, it is with no little pride that the editor writes these words of introduction. And it is appropriate, too, that thanks be extended to many individuals and institutions—the individual contributors, the editorial board, the American Revolution Bicentennial Commission of Connecticut, The Pequot Press, Mr. William Morris, Mr. George Mackie, Mrs. Judy Warfield, and Mr. David O. White, who has assumed responsibility for processing the illustrations for the entire series.

GLENN WEAVER
Editor
Bicentennial Commission
Publications

CONNECTICUT BICENTENNIAL SERIES I

Connecticut Joins the Revolution

By THOMAS C. BARROW

A Publication of
The American Revolution Bicentennial
Commission of Connecticut

Published by

PEQUOT PRESS

Chester, Connecticut

1973

Copyright © 1973 by The Pequot Press, Inc.

ISBN: 87106-123-6
Library of Congress Catalog Card Number: 73-83252
Manufactured in the United States of America
All Rights Reserved
FIRST PRINTING

Contents

Connecticut Joins the Revolution   7

Footnotes

Illustrations

    Jared Ingersoll   8
    King George III   10
    George Grenville   12
    Benjamin Franklin Cartoon   21
    Connecticut Courant Advertisement   21
    Citizens Demand Ingersoll's Resignation   24
    Resignation of Jared Ingersoll   25
    Frederick Lord North   39

Connecticut Joins the Revolution

IN the early years of the eighteenth century, the colony of Connecticut was the envy of its neighbors. Its famous charter gave Connecticut more self-government and political autonomy than the other colonies possessed. Its growth in resources and in population was noteworthy and without serious interruption. And its internal political and social life was so stable that Connecticut had become known as the "land of steady habits."

Of all the American colonies, Connecticut, seemingly, was the least likely to have serious complaints or objections to British rule. But when, after 1763, the problems and tensions between the colonies and Great Britain began to mount in intensity and seriousness, Connecticut was in the forefront of the movement which, within little more than one decade, would lead to American independence. How was it that the famous "land of steady habits" was so easily transformed into a leading participant in the rebellion against British rule?

The reasons were numerous. And the factors were complex. But two leading figures of eighteenth-century Connecticut, through their personal experiences and reactions, reflected in miniature, each in his own way, the general experiences of the people of Connecticut as a whole. For one of these men—Jared Ingersoll—the increasing friction between Britain and the colonies led to personal disappointment and tragedy. For the other—Jonathan Trumbull—the movement towards independence led to personal success and rapid advancement. In the careers and experiences of these two men—Jared Ingersoll and Jonathan Trumbull—lies the answer to how it came about that the colony of Connecticut, the famous "land of steady habits," joined the American Revolution.

Jared Ingersoll was a highly respected person within the colony of Connecticut. He was an American. And proud of it. But, a cautious and conservative man, Ingersoll also was a firm believer in the central importance of a proper respect for authority and for law and order. It was his commitment to the support of established authority that led Ingersoll to the single great mistake of his lengthy career.

For most of his life, Jared Ingersoll's conservative tastes and attitudes stood him in good stead. As a young man at Yale in 1741–1742, Ingersoll had made a favorable impression on some of the leading men in New Haven by declining to join in the efforts of the enthusiastic religious reformers who, at that time, were intent on introducing basic changes within the traditional religious practices and behavior of the

Jared Ingersoll. From Wyoming Historical and Geological Society, *The Susquehannah Company Papers*, IV.

colony. By his refusal to commit himself to the infectious enthusiasm of the evangelical religious revivalism associated with the "Great Awakening," Ingersoll made numerous life-long enemies. But, more importantly for the moment, he also made numerous friends. And the friends he made were influential and powerful enough to see to it that such a bright, articulate, and responsible young man as Ingersoll had an opportunity to make his way upward in the social and political life of colonial Connecticut.

The religious controversies that swept over the colony when Jared Ingersoll was a senior at Yale in 1742–1743 continued for many years. And the scars left behind lasted still longer. But Ingersoll reaped the benefits of his commitment to the orthodox religious system and the established social order of his day by receiving in 1758 the desirable appointment as the official representative or "agent" for Connecticut in England. Ingersoll's departure for London removed him from the controversies of his native colony and introduced him, to his great satisfaction and pleasure, to the cosmopolitan life of the capital city of one of the greatest countries and most powerful empires of that day.

Great Britain, in 1758, was in the midst of its climactic military conflict with its century-long enemy, France. Off and on, for some seventy years or more, England and France had gone to war in an effort to determine who would control the balance of power in Europe and who would obtain the greatest benefits from the settlement and conquest of colonial bases overseas. On the European continent, France, with its geographical position and manpower advantages, had the edge. But overseas, England, with its maritime strength and commercial interests, maintained an established superiority. The question involved in this climactic military contest was whether or not Britain could hold her own in Europe while she exploited her advantage overseas. Jared Ingersoll arrived in London at a critical movement in this conflict. And like most, if not all, Americans, Ingersoll, who not only took pride in his connection with England but who felt that Americans owed much to their continuing partnership within the framework of the British Empire, rejoiced in each and every English triumph.

The year 1759, the second year of Ingersoll's stay in London, was the famous "year of Miracles"—the *"annus mirabilis"*—of English history. Guadaloupe, the most prized of the islands in the West Indies, was captured by British imperial forces. In India, British military strength initiated the moves that led to the final expulsion of the French from the great sub-continent. But most important for Jared Ingersoll, and for all the American colonists, in 1759, Quebec, the heart of French North America, fell to the military genius of General James Wolfe. It would take several more years—four more years—before the terms of the peace treaty could be worked out. But by the close of the year

George III, British King during the American Revolution era. From Frank Arthur Mumby, *George III and the American Revolution*.

1759, it was obvious that the Great War for the Empire had been decided in favor of Britain. When a new young monarch—George III—came to the British throne in 1760, England's greatest imperial rival had been effectively eliminated from the North American continent. Not only in London, where Ingersoll joined in the celebrations, but throughout the British colonies in America and elsewhere, this triumphant conclusion to years of imperial rivalry and military conflict was a source of spontaneous and general rejoicing.

There were some men, very few, who had the foresight to see that the elimination of French power from North America had opened an entirely new chapter in the relationship between Britain and her colonies. Even during the war, both the English and the American colonists had found cause to complain about the performance of the other. From the American point of view, the British government had been willing to commit too few resources to the campaigns in North America and consequently had asked too much of them. From the English point of view, the Americans had shown too much willingness to carry on their usual business dealings with the enemy, particularly in the Caribbean Islands, and too great a reluctance to bear their share of the burden of the imperial military effort. Behind the joyfulness of the victory celebration lay a residue of distrust and resentment that was to play a major role in bringing Connecticut, and the other British North American colonies, to the point of rebellion.

Jared Ingersoll returned to New Haven in the fall of 1761. Fresh from the exhilaration of his years in London, he found that the controversies engendered by the religious differences of earlier years not only had persisted but had become part of the established political scene. Buy 1761, the "New Lights" (the party of the original religious evangelical reformers of the Great Awakening) had won control of the lower house of the Connecticut legislature. As one contemporary observer put it, by "their continued struggles," the New Lights had "acquired such an influence as to be nearly the ruling part of the Government owing to their superior Attention to Civil Affairs and close union among themselves in Politiks."[1] Ingersoll's enemies had made great gains politically during the years of his absence. And he had other opponents too, particularly various men interested in land speculation in Pennsylvania who felt Ingersoll had not worked for their cause as determinedly as he should have during his stay in London. The speculators involved in the Susquehannah Company's efforts to convert vague Indian deeds into profitable land investment outlets joined the "New Light" religious reformers in their distrust of Jared Ingersoll.

Had Jared Ingersoll remained nothing more than a colonial politician of local prominence, all these factors would have had only a minor importance in bringing Connecticut to the point of rebellion against the imperial rule of Britain. But, at a critical moment in relations

11

George Grenville, who introduced the Stamp Act to the House of Commons. From Frank Arthur Mumby, *George III and the American Revolution*.

between Britain and her American colonies, Ingersoll was called upon to play an influential role, particularly in Connecticut, in determining the outcome of the altered circumstances in which both the colonies and England found themselves after the close of the final imperial military struggle with France.

Ingersoll's important role, and eventually his personal political crisis, stemmed from the friendship he had made during his years in London with one of the most influential secretaries to the British Treasury Department, Thomas Whately. When the peace treaty between Britain and France finally was signed in 1763, the new prime minister, George Grenville, called upon Whately for help in devising financial reforms intended to oblige the American colonists to carry a larger share of the financial burden of governing and protecting the Empire. Specifically, Grenville had in mind a new tax—a stamp tax— which would oblige the colonists to pay for official stamps to be affixed to various commercial, legal, and general public documents. Suggestions for such a tax had been made many times earlier. But the new prime minister was determined to bring his own personal version of fiscal responsibility to the newly-enlarged Empire.

Already, in 1764, Parliament had passed the fateful Sugar Act, designed to tighten British control over the colonists' oceanic trade and to establish, once and for all, England's right to direct colonial economic and commercial development in the ways most advantageous to her own interests. These new restrictions came at a time when the colonists were suffering from the effects of a post-war economic depression. And, while the new restrictions were accepted in theory without too much open opposition, in practice this initial effort at increased imperial control met with a colonial reaction which ranged from reluctant obedience to open opposition.

Connecticut, with its charter and its relatively independent governmental and political process, was less directly affected by the Sugar Act and its new regulations than were the other colonies. Connecticut ports were important mostly in the local coastal trade. The nearest major oceanic port was Newport, Rhode Island. But most of the produce and general exports from Connecticut ports went either to New York or to Boston, where they were transferred for shipment to the West Indies, to Europe, or to other colonies. Consequently, the new English efforts at control of overseas trade were concentrated on New York, Boston, and Newport—the major ports of the northern colonial area. The Rhode Islanders were incensed enough by the new regulations to attack and burn one of the English vessels assigned to regulate their trade. In Massachusetts, the British officials found the local populace willing to use open force to block their efforts at enforcement of the Sugar Act. And in New York, the colonists used both open opposition and various legal maneuvers to obstruct enforcement of the new regulations of 1764. But Connecticut was affected only indirectly, and it was not until the Stamp Act was introduced that the people of that colony were led to serious open protest.

Ingersoll's English friend, Whately, wrote to ask his opinion of both the effects of the Sugar Act and the prospects for the proposed Stamp Tax. Ingersoll replied that the Sugar Act, and particularly the duty on molasses products imported into the colonies, imposed a greater burden than the colonists could afford to bear at that time. As for the proposed Stamp Tax, Ingersoll reported that the people of Connecticut, along with most colonists elsewhere, were alarmed at the prospect of new taxes imposed directly by Parliament and that it was an open question as to what the general colonial reaction would be should such a tax be introduced.

In 1764, by a fateful coincidence, Jared Ingersoll had occasion to sail for London in connection with a personal business affair. Consequently, he happened to be in England precisely at the moment when the crucial decision to introduce direct taxation of the American colonists was being made by Parliament. For Thomas Whately, and his other English friends, Ingersoll represented a legitimate spokesman for American interests and for the colonial point of view. Unfortunately for Whately, for Grenville, for the people of Connecticut, and for himself, however, Jared Ingersoll was only partially accurate in his understanding of the attitude and interests of his fellow colonists in Connecticut.

Connecticut in the mid-eighteenth century was an independent-minded colony with a population composed primarily of moderate-to-small landholders whose principal occupation was agricultural or, more rarely, land development and speculation. The people of Connecticut had much in common. A commonality of interest, and a similarity of life styles, combined with a relative degree of freedom from outside interference under their famous Charter, had made Connecticut in the early years of the eighteenth century a source of envy for some of her more politically and socially-divided neighbors. But by mid-century, the accumulated effects of the religious controversies which had come into the open during Ingersoll's years at Yale, coupled with other economic and commercial disagreements, had led to serious internal divisions within the former "land of steady habits."

One of the forces at work transforming Connecticut in the mid-years of the eighteenth century was its rapid growth in population. Accurate population figures for the pre-Revolutionary colonies are hard to come by. But according to the best available estimates, the total population of Connecticut more than tripled between 1730 and 1760. In 1730, the estimated population was 38,000; in 1749, it was 70,000. By 1760, it was over 130,000, and by 1774, it was close to the 200,000 mark.[2]

Included in the population figures for the year 1774 were 1,363 remnants of the once-numerous Indian tribes. More numerous by that date were the Blacks, who numbered some 5,101 and comprised roughly one-fortieth of the total population of the colony. Few, if any, of these Black colonists were free. Most were slaves, primarily located in the larger settlements such as New Haven, New London, and Stratford. Under the conditions of Connecticut's small-scale farming economy, the number of Blacks held in slavery by any one person was small, the average slaveholder owning only one or two. The slave's duties consisted either of household chores (in the larger towns) or of a variety of assignments within the diversified life of the colonial farm.[3]

Over the years, the various rivers of Connecticut played a major role in determining its patterns of settlement and population distribution. From the heavily-populated sections along the coast, lines of settlement spread northward from Stratford up the Housatonic and Naugatuck rivers to Waterbury, from New Haven northeast up to the Connecticut River Valley at Middletown and onward to the Massachusetts boundary, and from New London up the Thames River to Norwich.[4]

Not only did this pattern of settlement lead to a fairly even distribution of population across the colony, preventing any one section from dominating the others, but it also helped to keep the various towns roughly equal in size. Unlike some of the other colonies, Connecticut had no one city which, through its size and wealth, could overawe the others (as did Boston in Massachusetts; Newport and Providence in Rhode Island; and New York City in New York). The following table illustrates both the general growth and the relative standing of the major towns in Connecticut in the mid-eighteenth century:

TOWNS RANKED BY POPULATION

Towns Listed in Order of Rank by Population, 1774	1756 Census	1774 Census	Increase (per cent)
New Haven	5085	8295	63
Norwich	5540	7327	32
Farmington	3707	6069	64
New London	3171	5888	86
Stratford	3658	5555	52
Stonington	3518	5412	54
Woodbury	2911	5313	83
Hartford	3027	5031	66
Wallingford	3713	4915	32
Middletown	5664	4878	−14
Fairfield	4455	4863	9
Norwalk	3050	4388	44

15

The relative equality of distribution of population had been one of the sources of stability in the earlier "land of steady habits." But as the population increased, and as the agricultural resources failed to keep pace, ever larger numbers of the inhabitants began to demand more land and better economic opportunities generally. For a time in the 1730's, this desire for more land was satisfied by the public opening and sale of three hundred thousand acres of land in the northwestern section of the colony. But by 1750 the last of the colony's public lands had been taken up, and a number of colonists began to look outside the boundaries of Connecticut. A direct result of this interest in outside land speculation and development was the formation of the Susquehannah Company in 1753 in the town of Windham. The Susquehannah Company became not only a personal political problem for Jared Ingersoll, but also a major source of further controversy and division within the colony of Connecticut as well.

It was not a matter of coincidence that the Susquehannah Company was organized in the town of Windham. Located in the northeastern part of the colony, Windham, like other settlements in the eastern section, felt the pressures of declining land resources and growing population earlier than many other towns and areas. Consequently, it was more restless, less attached to things as they were, and more aggressive than other towns and other sections. Certainly, the people of Windham, and the other supporters of the new Susquehannah Company, were aggressive in their pursuit of official support for their efforts to obtain new lands for speculation and development outside the boundaries of Connecticut.

The original charter granted over a century earlier gave to the inhabitants of Connecticut a claim to extension of their boundaries to the further (Pacific) ocean. The charter had been given at an early date, when the true distance involved was unknown and when the area that later was to become New York was under Dutch control and before Pennsylvania had been settled, so that the extension of Connecticut's land claims to the west did not conflict with any existing *British* claims. But all this was of no importance to those in Connecticut who were interested in sharing in the open land available in the interior regions of the country. In 1754, the agents of the Susquehannah Company signed a treaty of dubious value with certain Indian chiefs in western Pennsylvania. If the British government could be persuaded to support the validity of this treaty—and it would require the full support of the governor and legislature of Connecticut to ensure the British approval—the investors in the Susquehannah Company would have title to land along the Susquehannah River in Pennsylvania. In fact, if approved, these investors would have title to practically the entire northern third of the colony of Pennsylvania. The stakes were large. And the supporters of the new Company were determined in their efforts to commit the government of Connecticut fully and formally to their project.

By 1765, the year the Stamp Act went into effect, the issue of the Susquehannah Company and its land claims in Pennsylvania had become a major source of controversy within the political life of Connecticut. The Governor, Thomas Fitch, represented the more conservative, more establishment-oriented, western coastal and interior towns. Consequently, he was opposed to the idea of involving the Connecticut government officially in the schemes of the Company, in part because he was fearful that the aggressive activities of the Company might lead the Crown to revoke the famous charter which allowed the colony so much self-government, and also because he himself and the interests he represented felt little urgent need for new lands for development or speculation. Jared Ingersoll shared Governor Fitch's feelings about the Susquehannah Company, and it was his failure to work actively in support of the Company's projects during the years he represented the colony in London that made Ingersoll an unpopular person in various sections and among certain groups within Connecticut.

But the Susquehannah Company was not without its backers. Ezra Stiles, the President of Yale College, estimated in 1763 that the Company "with their connections are large enough to influence one Third of the Votes in the Government, and might shake some out of the Council and Assembly."[5] Although in January, 1763, the British government specifically prohibited the Susquehannah Company from making any settlements in Pennsylvania for the immediate future, the adherents of the Company still did not surrender their hopes for persuading the British government to change its mind. So the issue of expansion outside the boundaries of the colony remained a source of controversy and bitterness within the political and social life of Connecticut.

The disagreements over the Susquehannah Company and its fortunes were a product of one of the changes that had transformed eighteenth-century Connecticut—the rapid increase in population and the consequent shortage of available agricultural land for development and investment. Fundamental changes also were taking place in the colony's general economic life and commercial relations with Britain. While these changes did not have the immediate and dramatic impact on the colony's political life that the Susquehannah Company did, still they added to the colony's problems and helped transform the former "land of steady habits" into a land of increasingly serious and bitter political divisions.

Mid-eighteenth-century Connecticut was a land of diversified, relatively small-scale farming. But in spite of the small size of its individual farms, Connecticut's agriculture was commercial, not merely subsistence, in its orientation. The farmers of Connecticut raised a variety of crops—corn (twenty to twenty-five bushels per acre), beans,

17

peas, squash, onions, apples, tobacco. And increasingly, after 1750, the raising of livestock (cattle, horses, mules, sheep, and hogs) occupied the time and the land of the colony's farmers.

But whether their produce was corn or apples, cattle or horses, it was produced not simply for home consumption but for export. The problem for mid-century colonial Connecticut in marketing its agricultural produce was two-fold—the colony had no major ocean ports of its own, and so was dependent on its neighbors' ports (New York and Boston primarily); and the one overseas area of the world with which it did have a direct and valuable trade—the West Indies—was increasingly closed to its shipping and trade as a result of the tightening of British regulations and imperial policies after the end of the war with France.

Connecticut's dependence on the ports of the neighboring colonies was caught in the perceptive remark of a traveler who visited the colony around 1760 and compared it "to a cask of good liquor, tapped at both ends, at one of which Boston draws, and New York at the other, till little is left in it but lees and settlings." This arrangement not only left Connecticut dependent on New York and Boston (and to a lesser extent, Newport and Providence) as a market for its agricultural produce, but also forced the people of Connecticut to rely on these ports as a source of the British manufactured goods they required. Consequently, the merchants of Boston and New York reaped the profits for acting as the "middleman" on both outgoing and incoming commercial transactions. Connecticut did better under this arrangement than the traveler's remark about the colony's being left only with the "lees and settlings" of the wine barrel would indicate, as attested by the general prosperous economic life of the colony up to 1760. Still, this dependence was a continual source of irritation to the people of Connecticut, who felt they were unfairly treated by their neighbors. Not the least of Connecticut's problems stemming from this relationship to its neighboring ports was the added complexity it brought to the general shortage of an established, stable currency within the American colonies.

As described in the words of the foremost authority on Connecticut in the pre-Revolutionary years, these trade arrangements, and particularly the shortage of money (either gold or silver, or a stable, generally acceptable paper currency), created a particularly vexing problem for the Connecticut merchant who

> . . . bought British goods on credit at Boston, Newport, and New York. The debtor interest created by this economic relationship was made more burdensome by the general money shortage in New England, which restricted the opportunities for the accumulation of capital and mercantile expansion. Under these circumstances the Connecticut trader was therefore likely, at times, to advocate a policy of moderate inflation.

Within the colony, however, the merchant sold his wares to Yankee farmers on credit, "Cash or Country Produce." His creditor interests in this relationship demanded a stable and dear [limited, more valuable] currency. The merchant's attitude toward the paper money question tended to vary, therefore, with his business needs and credit status in and outside the colony.[6]

The key to Connecticut's general prosperity and growth prior to 1760 was its overseas trade with the islands of the West Indies, both British and "foreign." Through the sale of its foodstuffs and livestock to these islands, Connecticut's merchants and farmers accumulated the specie and commercial credits which more than made up for the payments extracted from them by the "middlemen" in New York, Newport, and Boston. The effect of, and reaction to, the changes in English policy after 1763 which attempted to limit American trade to the West Indies was clearly expressed in the words of a member of one of Connecticut's leading commercial families:

> We must contrive some other Business than that to the W[est] Indies —as the Station [British guard] Ships prevent any Thing in the illicit Way [trade to non-British islands] and the Trade to the English Islands is much overdone. Indeed it seems hard that these Colonies should be mined to gratify the Avarice of a few individuals in England whose Interest lies in the W[est] Indies. . . .[7]

What the British government, through its policy changes at the end of the Seven Years' War, had done was to restrict, if not eliminate, the one single direct overseas market available to the people of Connecticut—a market which not only allowed them to escape the charges imposed on them by the "middlemen" in New York and Boston, but one which also brought home the gold and silver coins and the commercial credits they so desperately needed. It took time for the full implications of these changes in British policy to become apparent. And, prior to passage of the Stamp Act, Connecticut limited its protests to formal messages to Parliament in London. But the objections and the bitterness—aggravated by the post-war economic depression which reduced trade and profits—were gradually building in intensity. It took only the fateful enactment of the Stamp Act to bring this resentment into the open, as Jared Ingersoll was shortly to discover to his personal chagrin and lasting regret.

As Jared Ingersoll discovered through his own experiences, the post-war changes in British policy, particularly the ill-fated Stamp Act, had the effect of crystalizing the differences and heightening the divisions and controversies within Connecticut. The descendants of the earlier religious reformers, the "New Lights," who by 1765 controlled the lower house of the legislature, felt that the "Old Order" favored their opponents and perpetuated the control of the religious leadership and practices to which they took exception. The supporters of the Susquehannah Company and the idea of expansion beyond the boundaries of the colony continued to be restive under the continued reluctance of the governor of Connecticut and the legislature (and the British government) to press for recognition of their claims. And the commercial interests of the colony, including the market-oriented farmers, increasingly complained that the true interests of the colony were being ignored by the imperial authorities in London.

The opponents of the "New Lights," and of the Susquehannah Company—men like Jared Ingersoll—were aware of the unfortunate effect on Connecticut of the changes in British policy. But these men had a greater stake in the established order, and they were more reluctant to go too far in questioning the recognized authority of Great Britain. To do so, to question too openly and too forcibly the established authority of Britain, might lead to similar questioning by others of the established order and the authority of the existing government within Connecticut itself. These men were disturbed by the growing factionalism and controversies within their colony. No matter what the cost, they were reluctant to encourage any serious challenge to established authority by permitting overly radical or violent expressions of resistance to British policies.

It was for this reason that Jared Ingersoll, while he personally felt that the new English policies—particularly the Stamp Act—were opposed to the best interests of both his native Connecticut and all the other colonies, urged his fellow colonists to recognize the legitimacy of British authority and to obey the new laws, mistaken though they might be, while attempting to persuade the British government to reverse its disastrous policy decisions.

At this point in time, Ingersoll reflected the majority opinion of the inhabitants of Connecticut. When news of the proposed Stamp Act was officially communicated to them, the members of the Connecticut Assembly, with the support and consent of Governor Fitch, drew up an official protest which was forwarded to London. The opening section noted that it was their opinion that the "said Act for granting and applying certain Stamp Duties etc., as aforesaid, is unprecedented and unconstitutional." But the resolution went on to report that:

> "we look upon the well being and greatest Security of this Colony to depend (under God) on our Connections with Great Britain, which we ardently wish, may continue to the latest Posterity. And . . . that the Constitution of this Colony being understood and practised upon, as it has been ever since it existed, is the surest Bond of Union, Confidence, and mutual Prosperity of our Mother-Country and Us, and the best Foundation on which to build the good of the whole, whether considered in a civil, military, or mercantile Light. And of the Truth of this Opinion, we are the more confident as it is not founded on Specula-

Benjamin Franklin's famous 1754 political cartoon which first appeared in the *Pennsylvania Gazette*. Note that the New England colonies were placed together as a single unit. This cartoon was reproduced widely during the Stamp Act crisis.

THE laſt Tueſday of this Month (being the 25th Day) there is to be a General Congreſs of the SONS OF LIBERTY, in this Colony, to meet in Hartford, by their Repreſentatives choſen for that Purpoſe.

The patriotic and sometimes radical Sons of Liberty was organized in Connecticut and elsewhere in opposition to the 1765 Stamp Act. The meeting noted in this *Connecticut Courant* advertisement of March 10, 1766, led to the selection of candidates for governor and Connecticut's Upper House who advocated cooperation with the other American colonies.

tion only, but has been verified in Fact, and by long Experience, found to produce . . . as many loyal, virtuous, industrious, and well governed Subjects as any part of his Majesty's Dominions."[8]

The resolution respectfully requested a change of heart and of policy on the part of the British government. It was an appeal to reason and to long-standing traditions and relationships. And it contained no direct challenge to the established authority of Great Britain. At this stage in the growing crisis between Britain and her colonies, the people of Connecticut felt, as did Ingersoll, that the appropriate response was an appeal to reason and to tradition.

When Ingersoll arrived in England on personal business in 1764, the Stamp Act already had been drawn up but had not yet been enacted by Parliament. Ingersoll's friend, Thomas Whately, as chief secretary to the British Treasury, was in the process of reviewing the proposed Act for correction and revision. Ingersoll, along with other Americans then in London, did all they could to ameliorate the most objectional aspects of the new tax. According to reports, Ingersoll was at least partially responsible for persuading the British government to postpone the date the new tax would go into effect until November, 1765. And various items originally scheduled for taxation—such as marriage licenses and registers of ownership of vessels—were eliminated from the Act.

Having done what he could to remove some of the more objectional provisions from the Act, Ingersoll felt it would best serve the interests of his colony if a person already disposed in its favor—such as himself— were appointed as the official chiefly responsible for enforcement and collection of the new tax. On this point even such a prominent American as Benjamin Franklin was in agreement. Franklin helped to persuade Ingersoll that it would be both to his own personal interest and to the interest of his fellow colonists in Connecticut for him to accept appointment as collector of the Stamp tax. As far as the British government was concerned, appointment of such an established native of the colony seemed to guarantee the success of the new tax program there. So, the offer of the appointment was made to, and accepted by, Ingersoll, who returned to Connecticut in 1765 as the official representative of the British government charged with overseeing the effective operation of the fateful, new, direct tax on the American colonists.

Back in his native New Haven, Jared Ingersoll quickly discovered that he had underestimated the opposition of the people of Connecticut to the new tax. Although he attempted to persuade his fellow townsmen that the "Act is so contrived as to make it for your best interest to buy the stamps" and that when "I undertook the office I meant a service to you," nonetheless, at a town meeting on September 17 he was called upon, by a public vote, to resign his position as official stamp master. Ingersoll avoided a direct confrontation with the New Haven town meeting by declaring that he was not sure if he personally had the power to resign his royally-assigned responsibilities and that he preferred to wait "to see how the General Assembly is inclined."[9]

Ingersoll was aware that, without the support of the legislature and the colonial government, his position, even in New Haven, was untenable. And he knew that in other towns, particularly in the eastern sections of the colony where the "New Light" groups and the supporters of the Susquehannah Company were particularly strong, secret organizations which were coming to be called the "Sons of Liberty" were actively at work stirring up opposition to the Stamp Act across the entire countryside of Connecticut. Nevertheless, he hoped that the official, elected representatives of the people in the General Assembly would show more common sense and support him in his efforts to avoid a direct confrontation with British authority and power. So, shortly after the New Haven town meeting, Ingersoll set off for Hartford where the legislature was scheduled to meet.

For many of the miles between New Haven and Hartford, Ingersoll rode his horse alone and unmolested. But, as he neared Wethersfield, he began to encounter small groups of men. Eventually the groups grew in size, until, by the time he entered Wethersfield, his unasked-for escort numbered in the hundreds. Once in Wethersfield, it became clear that the crowd's intention was to force him to resign his post as collector of the stamp tax.

Ingersoll attempted to head off the demands for his resignation by telling the people of the town that the agitators were simply following the lead of the troublesome towns of the eastern part of the colony and that it seemed unfair "that the counties of New London and Windham should dictate to all the rest of the colony." But his attempted diversion failed, and shortly thereafter he was forced to shut himself up in a private home while the crowd outside waited for his decision. For three hours, Ingersoll delayed and negotiated. Apparently, he hoped to persuade the crowd, as he had the people of New Haven, that he could make no decision without consultation with the General Assembly and the governor. But he was not now at home in his native New Haven, and his audience was far less sympathetic. Finally, giving up hope of rescue or support, Ingersoll surrendered and signed an official statement of resignation from his office as collector of the stamp tax. Not content with this, the crowd forced Ingersoll to join them in shouting out their chosen slogan, "Liberty and Property." They then accompanied him all the way to Hartford, where he was required once again, in front of the legislature, to repeat his declaration of resignation and his commitment to the principles of "liberty and property." By giving in to the popular pressures for his resignation, Jared Ingersoll saved himself from further personal abuse and controversy. But his action, and his experiences during his short tenure of office as stamp

Jared Ingersoll, Royal Stamp Agent for Connecticut, and hostile citizens demanding his resignation on September 19, 1765. Wethersfield Historical Society photo.

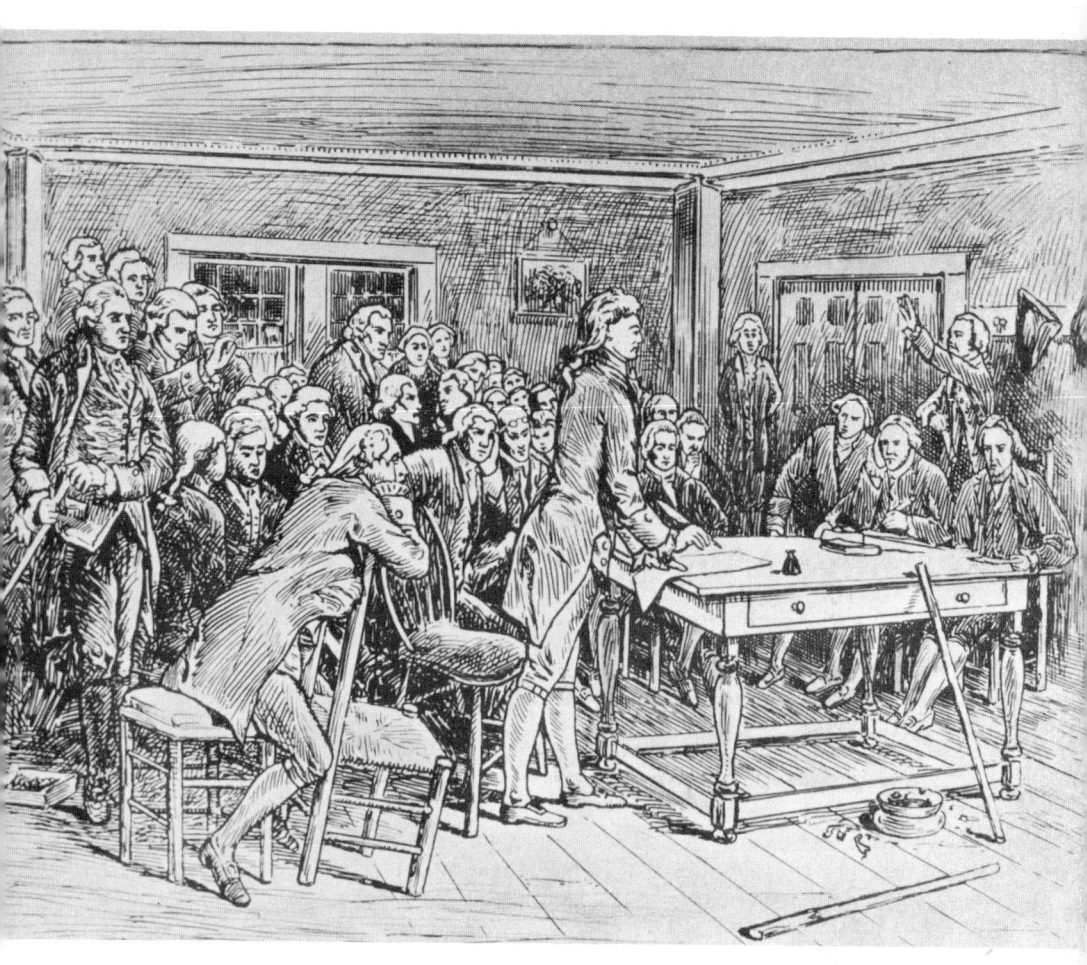

The resignation of Jared Ingersoll as Stamp Agent. Wethersfield Historical Society photo.

master, gave the supporters of British authority little cause for celebration or optimism.

The career of Jared Ingersoll, from his years at Yale through his bitter tenure of the office of stamp distributor, reflected in miniature and on a personal level the general experiences of the inhabitants of Connecticut in those troubled years. Divided among themselves by their increasingly-serious internal controversies and problems, the Connecticut colonists also were divided in their reactions to the new British imperial policies. The general unhappiness with the new policies provided the discontented and restless groups and factions within the colony with an irresistible opportunity to force the more conservative elements and sections to join them in open defiance of long-accepted authority. Quite naturally, much as they themselves might object to the turn taken by British imperial policies, the conservatives were reluctant to go too far too quickly for fear not only of losing their famous charter but also of further undermining the already-weakened respect for authority which supported what little remained of the happy memory of an earlier "land of steady habits." Just as it had for Jared Ingersoll personally, the Stamp Act precipitated a crisis within Connecticut generally by bringing these different views and interests into open confrontation with one another.

Jonathan Trumbull was a man of conviction and ambition. From the small, inland town of Lebanon in eastern Connecticut, Trumbull studied at Harvard and prepared for a career in the ministry. The death of an older brother brought about a change in plans, and Trumbull was needed to help his father with his business enterprises. In this way, Jonathan Trumbull became a merchant, and later a politician, instead of a minister. But throughout his career he retained much of the conviction, and some of the self-righteousness, he had acquired in his years of religious training.

Unlike Jared Ingersoll, Trumbull did not find a ready welcome waiting for him within the social and political establishment of Connecticut. From a small inland town, he had neither the more cosmopolitan background nor the more extensive social and political contacts that were available to Jared Ingersoll. And, coming from the eastern part of the colony, he did not fit naturally into the establishment group which came primarily from the west and which followed the lead of the governor, Thomas Fitch. But

> Jonathan Trumbull was determined to take his place in Connecticut's ruling class. His father, too, may once have had a similar ambition, but social success was not to come his way. Joseph Trumbull [the father] had been moderately prosperous in business and had won a place for himself in the affairs of church and town. In 1740 he built for himself a

nine-room dwelling in the style common to the homes of the well-to-do Connecticut farmers and merchants. In the Windham militia Joseph had risen to rank of captain and for two years acted as quartermaster for the Windham County troop, but those honors came only after he had passed his fiftieth year. Never had he been elected deputy to the General Assembly and never had he enjoyed appointment to one of the coveted colonial offices. Jonathan determined that *he* should not pass his life in obscurity.[10]

For many years, Jonathan Trumbull prospered in his commercial ventures, building on the base provided by his father and advancing within the commercial hierarchy from the rank of "inland distributor" to that of "importing merchant."[11] But the post-war depression after 1760 hurt him economically. And when trade failed to revive, and the shortage of money became even greater, Trumbull found himself seriously over-extended. His creditors forced him into bankruptcy in 1767. But, fortunately for Trumbull, by that date his political fortunes had risen as sharply as his financial resources had fallen, and he was able to survive his economic misfortunes. It was the fateful Stamp Act —the same Act that had put an effective end to Jared Ingersoll's rise within Connecticut's political structure—which opened the way for Trumbull to reach the very top of the political power structure of his native colony.

Thomas Fitch had been governor of Connecticut for a decade when the Stamp Act went into effect on November 1, 1765. A highly-respected lawyer, he had been one of the first men in Connecticut to point out the dangers inherent in the proposed new stamp tax. But, conservative by nature and firmly established within the existing social and political structure, like Jared Ingersoll, Governor Fitch was not inclined to oppose legitimate authority or laws. Consequently, once the Stamp Act became law, Fitch urged that it was his official duty as governor to support the enforcement of the new Act. In his view, the governor, and his councillors, were bound by "Allegiance . . . Office, and . . . Agreement or Contract, by accepting their Offices . . . to yield to the Requirements of the King and Parliament."[12] Defiance of British authority would jeopardize Connecticut's right to self-government and lead possibly to revocation of their Charter.

Consistent with these views, Governor Fitch resolved to take the required official oath to obey the Stamp Act. Had Ingersoll not resigned his position as stamp master, the governor would have supported him to the fullest possible extent. With Ingersoll gone, Fitch still was determined to fulfill his official responsibilities as he saw them. It was his intention to set an example of proper respect for the law and for established authority, no matter what his personal feelings about the Stamp Act might be.

Accordingly, Governor Fitch called together the members of the

Council to administer to him the official oath of obedience to the new law. A contemporary report has preserved what happened at that point: "A long debate ensued, finally the Gentlemen on the east side of the River refused, and withdrew." One of the councillors from eastern Connecticut who refused to administer the oath to the Governor was Jonathan Trumbull of Lebanon.

From the moment he refused to participate in the governor's pledge of support for enforcement of the Stamp Act, Jonathan Trumbull became a leading symbol within Connecticut of resistance to new imperial policies of Great Britain. Trumbull was not himself necessarily a radical, politically or socially. His views were reflected by his son, Joseph, who, as the Sons of Liberty became more active and established authority became more opened to question, wrote to his father: "It is dangerous to Write, or even Speak with Coolness now a days—whose Private Papers will next be demanded We can't tell—hope these things may soon Subside and that Order and regularity may Succeed the present Confusion."[13] But Trumbull's son was referring to the situation inside their home town of Lebanon, where they were the established leaders who had much to lose if the local radicalism went too far. Outside of the area of Lebanon, Jonathan Trumbull discovered that the popular uproar provided him with an opportunity to ensure that he would not pass his life in obscurity.

One of the results of the Stamp Act was that Connecticut did not stand alone in opposition to the new assertion by the British government of its imperial authority. After the passage of the Sugar Act in 1764, while the Stamp Act was still in its planning stage, the townspeople of Boston had made an appeal for united action against the new imperial policies:

> As his Majesty's other Northern American Colonys are embark'd with us in this most important Bottom, we further desire you to use your Endeavors, that their weight may be added to that of this Province; that by the united Applications of all who are Aggrieved, All may happily obtain Redress.[14]

In June, 1765, after receiving news of formal enactment of the Stamp Act, the Massachusetts legislature suggested a representative assembly of delegates from all the colonies to protest the new Act. Nine colonies responded, sending a total of twenty-seven representatives to the general gathering in New York City. This assembly, the Stamp Act Congress, was the first general, collective action ever initiated by the American colonists. And it established the working relationships which later produced the Continental Congress and the Declaration of Independence.

Some years earlier, a perceptive English visitor to the colonies had proclaimed that united action by the American colonists was a nearly total impossibility:

> A voluntary association or coalition, at least a permanent one, is [he wrote] . . . difficult to be supposed: for fire and water are not more heterogeneous than the different colonies in North-America. Nothing can exceed the jealousy and emulation which they possess in regard to each other. . . . In short, such is the difference of character, of manners, of religion, of interest, of the different colonies that I think . . . were they left to themselves, there would be a civil war; while the Indians and Negroes would, with better reason, impatiently watch the opportunity of exterminating them all together.[15]

Nor was this English visitor alone in his feelings. Such an experienced and partisan American as Benjamin Franklin, on the basis of his own efforts to bring about inter-colonial cooperation, had cause to comment: "Every Body cries, a Union is absolutely necessary; but when they come to the Manner and Form of the Union, their weak Noddles are presently distracted."[16]

Perhaps this general feeling was one of the prime reasons why, when American protests against the new policies first began to arrive in London, they were received with indifference and inattention. It was not simply that Parliament did not feel that it was necessary to repudiate the American protests. Worse, the British Parliament did not feel that it was necessary even to consider or answer those protests. Actually, Parliament had not rejected the American petitions; Parliament had simply refused to consider them at all, and thereby made painfully clear how much its members cared for the rights of the colonies.[17]

The American response, at least the response of many American colonists, was neatly summarized in the words of one New Yorker:

> When the Americans reflect upon the Parliament's refusal to hear their Representations—when they read abstracts of speeches . . . and find themselves condemned . . . and above all, when they see the prospects of innumerable loads arising from this connection with an overburdened nation interested in shaking the weight off of their own shoulders, and commanding silence in the oppressed Beast on which it is cast; what can be expected but discontent for a while, and in the end open opposition. . . . This single stroke has lost Great Britain the affection of all her Colonies.[18]

The people of Connecticut were not immune from such feelings. And, when the suggestion of sending delegates to an inter-colonial conference was received, the wish of the majority of the inhabitants was beyond dispute. Connecticut was determined to send its complement of delegates to the gathering in New York. But the followers of Governor Fitch and Jared Ingersoll still were strong enough to influence the directions given to the Connecticut delegation. Fearful that the representatives of the other colonies might prove to be more inclined toward radical measures than they themselves were, Fitch and his associates used their official positions and influence to ensure that the delegates to the New York assembly had no authority to pledge or bind Connecticut in any way whatsoever to the actions proposed by the Stamp Act Congress. The delegates were required to present their report and their recommendations to the General Assembly for its approval. In this way, Governor Fitch thought to counter in advance any possible extremist resolutions or actions stemming from the gathering in New York. Instead, Fitch shortly found his own legislature more than willing to endorse the results of the New York Stamp Act Congress; but he also unexpectedly discovered himself retired to private life after having served a decade as the chief executive of the colony of Connecticut.

The opening section of the Resolves drawn up by the intercolonial Stamp Act Congress was as temperate and respectful as Governor Fitch himself could have desired:

> The Members of this Congress, sincerely devoted, with the warmest Sentiments of Affection and Duty to his Majesty's Person and Government, inviolably attached to the present happy Establishment of the Protestant Succession, and with Minds deeply impressed by a Sense of the present and impending Misfortunes of the British Colonies on this Continent; having considered as maturely as Time will permit, the Circumstances of the said Colonies, esteem it our indispensible Duty, to make the following Declarations of our humble Opinion, respecting the most Essential Rights and Liberties of the Colonists, and of the Grievances under which they labour, by Reason of the late Acts of Parliament.

But the Stamp Act Congress resolutions went on, in section three, to declare that "it is inseparably essential to the Freedom of a People . . . that no Taxes be imposed on them, but with their own Consent, given personally, or by their Representatives." Since the British Parliament, through enactment of the Stamp Act, had clearly indicated its conviction of its established right to tax the colonists, that third section of the Stamp Act Resolves contained an implied, if not open, defiance of the authority of Parliament to levy taxes of *any* sort on the American colonists.

Like Jared Ingersoll, Governor Fitch made a fatal political miscalculation in regard to the public mood within Connecticut. Not only did he publicly urge the delegates to the Stamp Act Congress to denounce and disassociate themselves from the "excursions of the Giddy Populace"; but when he received the Resolves of the Congress, Fitch found them too aggressive for his tastes. He could not prevent the legislature from endorsing the Resolves, but he could, and did, inform the people of Connecticut that they had to accept the Stamp Act, "that forty men regulars could guard the Stamp papers, and that the American conduct would bring violent measures from home, and particularly the loss of Charter."[19] Such statements by Governor Fitch, coupled with his insistence on taking the official oath of obedience to the Stamp Act, not only led to his personal downfall but also brought to an end the long-established political dominance of Connecticut by the more conservative western towns.

The turning point in Connecticut's political life came with the election of 1766. From the spring of 1765 through the winter of 1766, popular agitation—spurred on by the Sons of Liberty, who took the lead from the towns of eastern Connecticut—increasingly shook the foundations of the established authorities within the colony. As Jared Ingersoll reported to his friend Thomas Whately in London, "no one dares, and few in power are disposed to punish any violences that are offered to the Authority of the Act—In short, all the springs of Government are broken and nothing but Anarchy and Confusion appear in Prospect."[20]

Actually, it was not anarchy or confusion, but a new political force that had come into being in Connecticut. Beginning as local groups created to focus public attention on the Stamp Act, the Sons of Liberty gradually were transformed into a colony-wide political organization whose purpose involved more than opposition to the Stamp Act. The main base for the Sons of Liberty was in the eastern towns. And some of their strongest support came from the "New Light" religious reformers and the advocates of the Susquehannah Company, both of which were strong in the east. The popular clamor against the Stamp Act allowed the easterners to ally themselves with opponents of the new British policies generally throughout the colony. The result was a colony-wide organization which showed its true strength in the election of 1766.

On March 25, 1766, a "General meeting of the Delegates of the Sons of Liberty, from a great majority of the towns" was held in Hartford. In response to a suggestion from the New York Sons of Liberty, this meeting established a standing "committee of correspondence" to keep in touch with their kindred groups in the other colonies. Once that matter was taken care of, by prearrangement, the eastern delegates called for a secret meeting "to collect the Minds of the People, for Unity, and by that Means be able to give the Freemen a Lead in the ensuing election, since, should they run upon different Men, the persons desired might not be elected, by the Freemen."[21] Some of the delegates were taken by surprise by his move to turn the meeting into a nominating convention for the upcoming election. But supporters of the plan were in the majority, in part because the "two Eastern Counties were much more generally attended than any other part of the government." It was decided to make nominations for the office of governor and deputy governor, but not for members of the Council (to avoid too much controversy). The delegates from the town of Litchfield dissented from this action, and the town of Hartford was divided in its reaction. But the success of the maneuver was proven on the second Thursday in May when, to the chagrin of Thomas Fitch and the satisfaction of the Sons of Liberty, the two leading councillors who had refused to administer the Stamp Act oath to Fitch—William Pitkin and Jonathan Trumbull—were elected governor and deputy governor, respectively.

For Trumbull, his election was a Godsend. As was customary, at the same time that he became deputy governor, Trumbull was also made chief justice of the Superior Court of Connecticut. The £100 salary he received as deputy governor was useful to him in his time of financial embarrassment. But, even more, his official positions enabled him to treat his creditors in a more independent and high-handed manner than would otherwise have been possible. When he was forced into bankruptcy in 1767, he was able to arrange matters to his own best advantage. Although he himself had been the author of the colony's strict laws regarding bankruptcy, Trumbull, as deputy governor, used his official position to work out a gentleman's agreement with his creditors, which left them only partially satisfied but which allowed him to keep much of his personal estate intact.

Trumbull had no hesitation in making such use of his new position. With good reason, he could claim that his economic reverses were not his own fault. In fact, Jonathan Trumbull's financial troubles were simply one part of the general economic difficulties of those years. Governor Fitch himself, in late 1765, had reported that trade in Connecticut was "at a very low Ebb through the Poverty of the People, the great Scarcity of Money, etc."[22] These economic hard times served to increase the anger of the colonists at the new British policies towards them. It was easy for the colonists to see themselves as victims of British greed and arrogance. And as victims, the colonists—like Trumbull personally—felt no reluctance in doing what they could to protect their own interests.

For a time, shortly after the election of Pitkin and Trumbull, the bitterness between the colonists and Great Britain receded. On the morning of May 19, a messenger arrived in New Haven "with the charming news that the obnoxious Stamp Act had been repealed by Parliament":

> The inhabitants were soon awakened with the banging of flintlocks throughout the town, bells rang madly, cannon volleyed; in the afternoon the people gathered in their churches where the clergy returned thanks for the blessing, after which the militia . . . appeared on dress parade; in the evening the rejoicing was concluded with illuminations, bonfires, and dances—all, as the chronicler carefully recorded [in the *Connecticut Gazette*], "without any remarkable indecency or disorder."

The celebration at Hartford four days later was less happy, if more spectacular. In the course of the rejoicing, "the large Brick School house was blown up with twenty-four white persons, two molattos, & two negro Boys." [23]

A combination of American protests, disorders in the colonies, and an effective boycott of British goods by American customers, had led Parliament to the action of repeal. Particularly the economic boycott, which reduced the value of imports from England from £1,925,664 in 1764 to £1,580,324 in 1765, and which led English merchants to join in appealing for an end to the controversial Stamp Tax, persuaded the British government to change its mind. None of the hated stamps had been sold in Connecticut. Five shipments of official stamps had been sent out to the colony from England; but, except for some that were burned in popular protest, all the stamps remained in a fort in New York until in mid-summer of 1766, on the instructions of Jared Ingersoll, they were shipped back to England.

Parliament repealed the Stamp Act. But along with the repeal of that Act, Parliament also enacted the Declaratory Act, which was intended to "save face" for the British government by asserting its theoretical supremacy over the colonists. The Declaratory Act stated:

> That the said colonies . . . have been, are, and of right ought to be, subordinate unto, and dependent upon the imperial crown and parliament of Great Britain; and that . . . parliament . . . had, hath, and of right ought to have, full power and authority to make laws and statutes of sufficient force and validity to bind the colonies and people of America, subjects of the crown of Great Britain, in all cases whatsoever.

While willing to concede the inexpediency of attempting to enforce the Stamp Act, the British government maintained its claims to imperial authority. And it was not long before a new test of strength developed between the colonists and the mother country. In January, 1767, a member of the British ministry, Charles Townshend, announced that he knew how to raise money in the American colonies without angering the colonists. Still annoyed by the American resistance to the ill-fated Stamp Act, the majority of the members of Parliament decided to take Townshend at his word and asked for the details of his plan. The result was passage of the Townshend Acts of 1767.

The main act in Townshend's program was a new revenue measure, levying duties on glass, lead, tea, paint, and paper imported into the American colonies. Townshend's argument was that, in protesting the Stamp Act, the colonists had objected only to taxes levied *within* the colonies. His new duties were to be collected at the time of entry, and, consequently, were external rather than internal taxes. Therefore, there should be no reason for Americans to object as they had to the Stamp Tax. Supplementing this taxation measure was another act creating

33

a special Board of Customs Collectors, to reside in Boston, who were charged with overseeing the collection of the new duties as well as general colonial obedience to the commercial regulations laid down by Parliament.

The Townshend duties were not heavy and were intended to raise only some £40,000 a year. But Townshend's hope was to increase these taxes gradually, once they were accepted, until a sufficient fund would be available to the British government not only to save it from spending its own money to maintain its hold on the colonies, but also to enable it to strengthen its control of the governments and people of the various colonies. The proceeds of the new duties were to be applied, not to the upkeep of the army or the navy as had been the intention under the Sugar and Stamp Acts, but rather to "defraying the charges of the administration of justice, and the support of the civil government, within all or any of the said colonies or plantations."

The amounts of money involved were small. And the general American reaction to the Townshend Acts was slow in taking shape. But, alerted by their experience with the Stamp Act, the leaders of the colonial opposition well understood the full implications of the new program. As Jonathan Trumbull reported, it was his fear that the new taxes would be used for the:

> support of Tax gatherers and their Numerous Train, for rendering Governors and Judges independent of the people for their Support, and for the maintenance of Troops in the Colonies, to Overawe them to Compliance with things grievous and hard to be born.[24]

Such a threat had particular meaning and significance in the charter colony of Connecticut, with its long tradition of relative self-government and self-determination. As Governor Pitkin warned the British government, "Bare naked power is an awful thing and very unamiable to a people that have been used to be free." How far the divisions between the colonists and Great Britain had gone was indicated in the warning of another Connecticut man to the British government: should the British attempt to force the issue, "our Blood is more at their service than our Liberties."[25]

Recalling the success of the economic pressures exerted on England during the Stamp Act crisis, political leaders in Boston, New York, and Philadelphia urged the American colonists to refuse to import or to buy English goods. Again, the eastern towns in Connecticut were the first to take action; but by May, 1768, the General Assembly indicated its full support of the boycott by levying a special 5% duty on goods brought into Connecticut by non-resident merchants. Shortly thereafter, the merchants of the colony joined their colleagues in Boston and elsewhere by subscribing to the non-importation agreement, thus, in the words of the lower house of the legislature, "sacrificing their private fortunes to the cause of liberty."

Special "committees of inspection" (unofficial committees, like the Sons of Liberty) applied public pressure to merchants who were reluctant to join the boycott. Offending merchants found their names published in the newspapers and were denounced at town meetings. Once again, the unofficial authority of these "citizen groups" was sufficient to bring the commercial importers and retailers under control.

This time, however, the British government surprised the colonists. A change in the political situation in London brought a new prime minister, Lord North, to power. Even before he assumed power, and even before the non-importation agreements were implemented, the British government had experienced second thoughts about the Townshend-tax program. The small returns from the new taxes, coupled with the opposition they aroused, led the ministry in 1768 to debate repeal. The problem was how to withdraw gracefully from their latest failure to assert their authority over their recalcitrant colonists. The answer, proposed by Lord North and approved by Parliament, was to repeal all the duties imposed by the Townshend Acts except that on tea.

This unexpected retreat by the British government left the leaders of the colonial opposition in Connecticut and the other colonies in an awkward position. The merchants of New York City were the first to accept the action taken by Lord North as satisfactory and to resume the importation of English products. At first, the merchants of Connecticut were highly critical of this defection by the New Yorkers before complete and final repeal of all the Townshend Acts had been achieved. But shortly, in spite of all the efforts of the committees of inspection and others, the merchants of Connecticut tentatively began to bring British imports into the colony from the neighboring city of New York. And, despite newspaper appeals, the people of Connecticut began to purchase the English goods. The trickle became a stream, and the stream soon became a flood of English products. Commenting on the changed situation, one Connecticut observer bemoaned the fact that "It looks as tho the Country would again be filled with Goods and Deludged in Debt. Thus has the boasted Patriotism of our Merchants been conquered by all powerful Interest!"[26]

By this time, Jonathan Trumbull's political fortunes had improved to the point that he was no longer dependent on his commercial activities. In 1769, William Pitkin died, and Trumbull became governor of Connecticut. From that time until his voluntary retirement in 1783, because of advanced age, Jonathan Trumbull was continually reelected to the office of chief magistrate. Perhaps without the fateful intervention of the Stamp Act and the changes that occurred in relations between the people of Connecticut and the mother country, Jared Ingersoll would have progressed naturally and uneventfully to that high office. But

Ingersoll's attitudes and personal ambitions led him astray. Accepting the position of Stamp Master, Ingersoll, and those of his persuasion, lost the confidence of the people of his colony. The door was opened for others more closely attuned to the changing times and the growing restiveness of the people of Connecticut under British rule. By past experience and personal interest, Jonathan Trumbull, and those of *his* persuasion, identified themselves more closely with the new attitudes and interests of their fellow colonists. So it was that a new order came to Connecticut, and Jonathan Trumbull served as governor during the transition of his native colony to independence and statehood under the Articles of Confederation.

But, in his new position as governor, Trumbull at first had to exercise caution and common sense. With the repeal of the majority of the Townshend duties, a period of renewed good will towards England was evident within Connecticut. But at the same time, the internal tensions and problems that plagued the colony for a generation still persisted. Added to the division between "New Light" and "Old Light" Congregationalists was a concern on the part of the established Congregational ministers at the continued growth of the Anglican Church within the colony. In the view of Ezra Stiles, one of the most prominent religious leaders in Connecticut, the "Stamp Act, Episcopal Hierarchy, and military Government were all branches of the same Policy or Grenvillian System of Plantation Colony Dominion." The response of the Anglicans was the angry complaint that the very same men who were so insistent on their own rights in opposition to British authority had little respect for the rights of others: "Thus the violent asserters of civil liberty for themselves, as violently plead the cause of tyranny against ecclesiastical liberty to others." The outspoken opposition to their church led some Anglicans to fear the worst: "God have Mercy upon us if the Provinces here should throw off their connection, dependance and subjection to the Mother Country."[27]

The divisions within Connecticut remained. And the colony over which Trumbull presided was no longer the former "land of steady habits." The Susquehannah Company issue, too, still divided the colony. The victory of the eastern sections with the election of Trumbull naturally led supporters of the Company to expect more active commitment from the legislature and government to the cause of their land claims in Pennsylvania. Jonathan Trumbull, a member of the Company for many years, was in an ideal position to further its prospects. Consequently, the Company's supporters looked to him for positive results. Equally, opponents of the Company looked upon Trumbull with suspicion. At stake was not just the fate of the Susquehannah Company, but also the much larger question of Connecticut's relations with both England and its fellow colony of Pennsylvania. To push the Company's claims would not only involve the colony with the British government but also with the proprietary colony of Pennsylvania. Supporting the Company at the possible costs of a split with both London and Philadelphia was not an attractive prospect to many people in Connecticut.

These and other problems made the election of 1770 one of the most bitterly-fought political contests in Connecticut's colonial history. For the conservative western towns, and their allies, it represented a last stand against the alliance that had brought first Pitkin and then Trumbull to the office of governor. Thomas Fitch was still the leader of this group, and he was Trumbull's principal opponent in this crucial election. The spirit of the conservatives' campaign was communicated effectively in the anti-Trumbull ballad they circulated widely (in the ballad, "Will" stands for Pitkin; the "Purser" is Trumbull; and "old Pitch" is, of course, Fitch):

> Now Will is dead and his Purser broke
>   I know not who'll come next, Sir;
> The Seamen call for old Pitch again,—
>   Affairs are sore perplexed, Sir,
>
> But the Gunners and some midshippers
>   Are making an insurrection,
> And would rather the ship should founder quite
>   than be saved by Pitch's inspection.
>
> But this is what I will maintain,
>   In spite of Gunners and all, Sir,—
> If Pitch can save the Ship once more,
>   'Tis best he overhaul her![28]

Trumbull's supporters responded with charges that their opponents were all former partisans of the Stamp Act and of increased British interference with Connecticut's traditional liberties. But underneath, the religious, commercial, and geographic divisions all played their part in this critical election year.

Trumbull's victory in this bitter election cemented his hold on the governorship. It also established on a lasting basis, the influence of the alliance that had come to power in the Stamp Act year of 1766. Fittingly, Jared Ingersoll, who once had looked forward to such a brilliant future within his native Connecticut, in 1770—the year of Trumbull's triumph—accepted a royal appointment as judge of the British Vice-Admiralty Court for the Middle Colonies and left for Philadelphia. Ingersoll was to maintain his ties to Connecticut, and when he died in 1781, his home town, New Haven, marked his passing with due respect and regret. But Ingersoll had failed to change with the changing times that were transforming his colony. He had become a symbol of older times even before he made the final move to his new home in Philadelphia.

For Trumbull, the years immediately following the election of 1770 were a time of careful maneuvering and skillful adjustment. The repeal of the major Townshend Duties, and the collapse of the non-importation agreements, made it abundantly clear that the people of Connecticut, like the majority of the colonists everywhere, were eager for, and hopeful of, a final end to the decade of tension and controversies between Britain and the Americans. It was a time for moderation in all things, particularly in government.

During this time, the issue of the Susquehannah Company grew ever more serious. Trumbull used his influence to get the colonial government officially committed to the support of the Company's claims. Gradually, the supporters of the Company made headway. The British authorities were reluctant to get too involved in an inter-colonial dispute between Connecticut and Pennsylvania, and the advocates of the Company took this British restraint as a sign of approval. Trumbull himself connected the success of the Company's claims to land in Pennsylvania with the issue of Connecticut's future relationship to the other colonies. Without room for growth, Connecticut would increasingly be at a disadvantage in dealings with those colonies like New York and Pennsylvania which had vast lands still to be developed. It was an effective appeal. And by 1774, the entire colony was once again divided over the issue of the Susquehannah Company and its fortunes.

Fortunately for Trumbull, just as the internal controversy over the Susquehannah Company was reaching its peak, once again a dramatic change in British imperial policies introduced a new and distracting element into Connecticut politics. By 1773, the great British East India Company was in financial distress. Many influential men in England were involved in this Company, and its fiscal difficulties were of basic concern to the British government. The Company depended heavily on income from its marketing of tea from the Far East; but the economic hard times and an over-supply of tea had left the Company's warehouses full of unsold, rotting tea, while its stock dropped daily in value on the London Exchange. New markets were needed quickly, and the prospect of increasing the sale of tea within the colonies was too great a temptation for the usually cautious Lord North. The Prime Minister saw, or thought he saw, a way both to increase the sale of tea *and* to collect additional tax revenues within the American colonies. By permitting the East India Company to ship tea directly to the colonies, instead of requiring the tea to be shipped through England as formerly, Lord North could arrange it so that the Company's expenses would be reduced and it could sell its tea for less money, with a consequent rise in sales. At the same time, since the only remaining tax duty from the original Townshend Acts was the tax on tea imported

Frederick Lord North, British Prime Minister. From Frank Arthur Mumby, *George III and the American Revolution.*

into America, the increased sale of tea automatically would lead to an increase in tax collections there.

Lord North's plan was clever. But he made one basic mistake. Like his predecessors, he underestimated the Americans' awareness of the importance of the issue of taxes of any kind imposed on them solely and simply at the will and discretion of Britain. Unwittingly, Lord North made the importation of tea even more of a symbol than the stamp tax had been of the conflict of interests between Britain and the colonies. And, in doing so, he initiated the final steps that brought the colonies, and Connecticut, to the point of Revolution.

As in the case of the earlier Townshend Acts, Connecticut's reaction to the new Tea Act was somewhat slow in developing. Most tea imports came directly into Boston or New York, not into Connecticut ports. So the initial test of the reaction of the colonists logically could be expected in those cities. A poetically-inspired Connecticut patriot called upon the people of Boston to take appropriate action:

> Parliament an Act has made
> That will distress and ruin trade,
> To raise a Tax as we are told,
> That will enslave both young and old;
> Look out poor Boston, make a stand,
> Don't suffer any Tea to land.[29]

But in this case the call to action was late. Already the shipments of tea arriving in Boston Harbor had been dumped into the ocean. And the full weight of Britain's imperial anger was about to descend on her American colonies.

The reaction within Connecticut to the Boston Tea Party was predictable. Conservatives, and those who still clung to the hope of an end to controversies between the colonies and Britain, were distraught. Those who mistrusted English intentions, along with those who had profited from the changes that had taken place in Connecticut's political life and structure since the inauguration of the controversial new imperial policies, were eager to make the most of the new Parliamentary enactment.

At this crucial juncture, the British government once again played into the hands of the anti-British factions within Connecticut and the other colonies. The punishment inflicted on Boston was the passage of the Coercive Acts. In the first of its retaliatory acts, Parliament on March 25, 1774, closed the port of Boston to all shipping until its citizens paid the East India Company for the lost tea. Later, in May and June, three more Acts were added. The Massachusetts Governing Act brought an end to charter government in that colony. The Quartering Act permitted the forceful quartering of British troops wherever necessary. And the Administration of Justice Act permitted British soldiers, administrators, or customs officials charged with offenses committed while on duty to have their court cases transferred to another colony, or to England, whichever was necessary to ensure them of a fair trial. In explaining these harsh measures, Lord North proclaimed that it now was no longer a question of taxation but of whether or not Britain retained any authority whatsoever over the "haughty American republicans." The king announced that "We must master them or totally leave them to themselves and treat them as aliens."[30] Clearly, the British felt that the time had come for a final test of strength with their recalcitrant colonists. The American response quickly made it apparent that they were more than ready for the challenge.

The Massachusetts Committee of Correspondence, in answer to the Coercive Acts, called upon all the other colonies to rally to their support by breaking off all trade with Great Britain. The town meeting of Boston sent a similar appeal to its sister ports in the other colonies, stating that if, by a policy of non-importation, "the Act for Blocking up this Harbor be repealed, the same will prove the salavation of North America and her Liberties."[31]

On May 23, the town meeting of New Haven considered the Boston letter and voted to defend "the liberty and immunities of British America" to their utmost ability. Five days later, the Virginia House of Burgesses adopted resolutions in favor of an annual inter-colonial congress on the model of the earlier Stamp Act Congress. Within Connecticut, Silas Deane, a member of the colony's Committee of Correspondence, was already in favor of such action. As Deane explained it, local non-importation and non-purchase agreements were of some use, but were likely to be of varied effectiveness from community to community and also were likely to be productive of mutual suspicion and distrust. In June, the colony's legislature took the unusual step of officially empowering the Committee of Correspondence to select delegates to represent Connecticut at the new inter-colonial congress. By this action, it was ensured that the delegates would be comprised of dedicated opponents of British authority. As a charter colony itself, with a long tradition of self-government, Connecticut was particularly mindful of the fate that had befallen the people of Massachusetts. What had happened there could happen elsewhere. And it well might happen elsewhere unless the colonies were united in their resistance to the Coercive Acts. Three staunch "Patriots"—Roger Sherman, Eliphalet Dyer, and Silas Deane—were selected to attend the First Continental Congress.

Throughout the summer and fall of 1774, the Whig "Patriots" worked hard to silence their Tory opponents and to win over the fence-sitters.

During the summer and fall of 1774 the supposedly sober people of

Connecticut took matters into their own hands with increasing frequency. Radicals in Mansfield and Ashford cooperated to induce a resident of the latter town to confess that he had been grievously wrong to speak against the "charter-rights of the American colonies." ... Similar dramatic incidents took place in other towns. Zealous Whigs compelled Tories to suffer penance for such political crimes as not attending liberty-pole celebrations.... Captain Hezekiah Whittelesey, one of Saybrook's deputies, was one of those whose opinions were considered highly obnoxious. A large number of Liberty Boys duly visited him ... and convinced him of the serious errors he had committed....[32]

In Fairfield and Newtown, rioting mobs sought out the property of suspected Tories. And even in conservative New Haven, the Patriots organized a "Committee of Friends of Constitutional Liberty" who, according to the Tory opponents, did all they could to encourage "mobs, riots, and unjustifiable outrages." Even had he wished to do so, Governor Trumbull could not have stopped these excesses. The mood of the people of the colony was angry. And all that would be needed to turn that anger into open rebellion was a spark. Very shortly, further news from Massachusetts provided that spark, and Connecticut joined the other colonies in revolution.

Meeting in Philadelphia, the First Continental Congress rejected the right of Parliament to tax the colonists and recommended immediate steps to establish an effective inter-colonial machinery of resistance. These measures added to the patriotic ardor and determination of the Whig partisans. Then on Wednesday, April 19, the shots heard round the world were fired at Lexington and Concord. By the next afternoon, the news had spread through Connecticut. A special session of the General Assembly was hastily called together. A quarter of the available militia were ordered into service. A special emission of £50,000 worth of bills of credit was authorized. And arrangements were made to purchase arms and ammunition. Connecticut was on the verge of war.

Governor Trumbull was experienced enough politically to do his best to convince his people that the blame for Lexington and Concord—and whatever followed—was entirely the responsibility of the British. In a skillfully-written letter to General Gage, the military governor of Massachusetts under the authority of the Coercive Acts, Trumbull set out the expected statements of Connecticut's determination to stand by its embattled neighbor and to protect its own rights. But, in an additional comment, he gave Gage an opportunity to make his position clear. Admitting that "we are not sure of every part of our information," Trumbull requested an explanation of the general's intentions. At the same time, he suggested that Gage should "suspend the operations of war," which would enable him to "quiet the minds" of the people of Connecticut, "at least till the result of some further deliberations may be known."[33] In this way, Governor Trumbull effectively put the responsibility for any further confrontations or hostilities squarely on the shoulders of General Gage. And it enabled Trumbull to display his moderation and reasonableness for all the fence-sitters in Connecticut to see.

But General Gage was under orders. And the British government was in no mood to back off at this point from a trial of strength with the colonists. And the attitude of the people of Connecticut in the months after Lexington and Concord was eloquently summarized in the Reverend Judah Champion's election day sermon in May, 1776:

> For Heaven's sake and for our own . . . act up to the dignity of our character as free-born Americans . . . by all that Christ hath done and suffered to purchase our privileges and eternal salvation . . . by all your regard to the sacred Trinity, to yourselves, to posterity, and to your country, we beseech and adjure you to *Stand fast in the Liberty wherewith Christ hath made us free.*[34]

By the date of this sermon, the British troops had evacuated Boston, General Washington was preparing for an expected descent by British troops on New York City, Tom Paine had presented his argument for American independence—*Common Sense*—and the defense of American "Liberty" had become inseparable from independence. The American Revolution was in full progress, with the whole-hearted support and commitment of inhabitants of the formerly loyal "land of steady habits" —the former colony, and future state, of Connecticut.

Jared Ingersoll, once a rising member of Connecticut's political and social establishment, died in August, 1781, less than two months before the decisive American victory at Yorktown. From the time of his acceptance of the appointment as Stamp Master in 1765, Ingersoll had tried valiantly to reconcile his personal convictions and training with the changing world of his native colony. But it was not to be:

> A lonely and repudiated champion of the old order of things which was passing away before his eyes never to return, he yet sought to adjust himself to the new conditions. "But all this made him unhappy," in the words of his friend, Ezra Stiles; his soul had become a battle ground and he wearied of life.[35]

Had he lived, Ingersoll might well have been amused by the farewell message Governor Jonathan Trumbull issued to the people of Connecticut on the occasion of his voluntary retirement from office in 1783. On the basis of Ingersoll's experiences, Trumbull was a leading representative of the forces working to undermine respect for authority and appreciation of the need for order. Yet in his farewell message, Trumbull urged his fellow citizens to "pay an orderly and respectful regard to the laws and regulations of government." Particularly Ingersoll might have noted how Trumbull, who himself had made such good use of the opportunities opened to him by the controversies that plagued Connecticut after 1763, deplored contention and divisiveness: "my fellow citizens, I exhort you to love one another: let each one study the good of his neighbor and of the community, as his own:—hate strifes, contentions, jealousies, envy, avarice, and every evil work, and ground yourselves in this faithful and sure axiom, that virtue exalteth a nation, but that sin and evil workings are the destruction of a people."[36]

But Ingersoll would have been wrong. Trumbull was not dishonest. Nor was he a hypocrite. In 1783, he simply was defending and extolling the *new* established order in which he played such a central role. In Trumbull's place, Ingersoll would have, as he did in defending the established order of the pre-1763 Connecticut into which he was born, done precisely the same.

The question was not who was the better man or whose ideals were higher. The question was, as it must be in any democratic society, which man more closely reflected and understood the world in which he lived. Mid-eighteenth-century Connecticut was a world in change. As its population grew, so did its problems and its complexities. The "land of steady habits" that produced Jared Ingersoll was a simpler world, less complicated and less controversial. By 1750, colonial Connecticut had outgrown its earlier simplicity. Only with difficulty had Ingersoll's predecessors within the establishment held their position and authority. Unfortunately for them, changes also were taking place in England. New ministers, new imperial policies, brought on a contest of wills between the Mother Country and the colonies. In the process, the rate of change within Connecticut was speeded up. The new interests, the new political and social forces, were provided with an opportunity to couple their aspirations with those of an increasing number of their fellow colonists.

The answer to the question of how it happened that eighteenth-century-Connecticut came to join in the Revolution is, simply, that both Connecticut and England outgrew the simpler relationships of earlier, more happy days. Connecticut was a rapidly growing society, a society of increasing inner complexity and problems. At a crucial moment, the Mother Country—like Ingersoll—displayed a fatal lack of understanding of that growth and change. By instinct, intelligence, and interest, Jonathan Trumbull understood what Ingersoll—and England—did not. He understood that it was time for a change in relations between the colonies and the Mother Country. And it was that understanding that brought Trumbull to the office of governor. It was a similar understanding, and desire, on the part of his fellow citizens of the former "land of steady habits" that brought them, and Connecticut, to join the American Revolution.

Notes

1. Edmund S. and Helen M. Morgan, *The Stamp Act Crisis: Prologue to Revolution* (New York, 1965), 289.
2. Oscar Zeichner, *Connecticut's Years of Controversy, 1750–1776* (Williamsburg, 1949), 29–30.
3. Albert E. Van Dusen, *Connecticut* (New York, 1961), 110.
4. Van Dusen, *Connecticut,* 105.
5. Zeichner, *Years of Controversy,* 34.
6. Zeichner, *Years of Controversy,* 38–39.
7. Zeichner, *Years of Controversy,* 42.
8. C. J. Hoadley, ed., *Public Records of the Colony of Connecticut* (Hardtford, 1850–1890), XII, 421–425.
9. G. H. Hollister, *The History of Connecticut,* 2 vols., (Hardtford, 1857), II, 133.
10. Glenn Weaver, *Jonathan Trumbull, Connecticut's Merchant Magistrate (1710–1785)* (Hartford, 1956), 25.
11. Weaver, *Trumbull,* 54.
12. Zeichner, *Years of Controversy,* 58.
13. Zeichner, *Years of Controversy,* 65.
14. Morgan, *Stamp Act,* 138.
15. Andrew Burnaby, *Travels Through the Middle Settlements in North America in the years 1759 and 1760* (Ithaca, New York, 1960), 110–114.
16. *The Papers of Benjamin Franklin,* Leonard W. Labaree, ed., 15 vols. to date (New Haven, 1959–   ), V. 452.
17. Morgan, *Stamp Act,* 120.
18. Morgan, *Stamp Act,* 121.
19. Zeichner, *Years of Controversy,* 57.
20. Lawrence Henry Gipson, *American Loyalist: Jared Ingersoll* (New Haven, 1971), 195.
21. Gipson, *Ingersoll,* 219.
22. Zeichner, *Years of Controversy,* 59.
23. Gipson, *Ingersoll,* 225.
24. Zeichner, *Years of Controversy,* 84.
25. Zeichner, *Years of Controversy,* 85.
26. Zeichner, *Years of Controversy,* 87.
27. Zeichner, *Years of Controversy,* 98.
28. Zeichner, *Years of Controversy,* 123.
29. Zeichner, *Years of Controversy,* 160.
30. David Hawke, *The Colonial Experience* (Indianapolis, 1966), 563.
31. Gipson, *Ingersoll,* 328.
32. Zeichner, *Years of Controversy,* 172–173.
33. Zeichner, *Years of Controversy,* 192–193.
34. Zeichner, *Years of Controversy,* 210–211.
35. Gipson, Ingersoll, 376.
36. I. W. Stuart, *Life of Jonathan Trumbull, Sen., Governor of Connecticut* (Boston, 1859), 608.

A5